Alcohol

DEBORAH CHANCELLOR

W
FRANKLIN WATTS
LONDON • SYDNEY

First published in 2009
by Franklin Watts

Copyright © Franklin Watts 2009

Franklin Watts
338 Euston Road
London NW1 3BH

Franklin Watts Australia
Level 17/207 Kent Street
Sydney, NSW 2000

Series editor: Sarah Peutrill
Editor: Sarah Ridley
Art director: Jonathan Hair
Design: www.rawshock.co.uk
Picture researcher: Diana Morris

Dewey number: 362.292

ISBN 978 0 7496 8833 2

Printed in Malaysia

Franklin Watts is a division of Hachette Children's
Books, an Hachette UK company.
www.hachette.co.uk

CONTENTS

Look out for these features

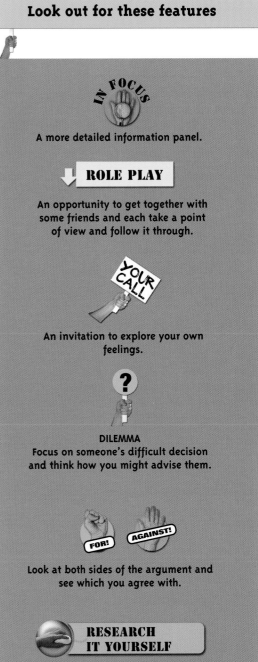

IN FOCUS

A more detailed information panel.

ROLE PLAY

An opportunity to get together with some friends and each take a point of view and follow it through.

YOUR CALL

An invitation to explore your own feelings.

?

DILEMMA
Focus on someone's difficult decision and think how you might advise them.

FOR! **AGAINST!**

Look at both sides of the argument and see which you agree with.

RESEARCH IT YOURSELF

Some topics that you could research yourself, either in the library or on the Internet.

What is alcohol?

Alcohol is the world's most common drug. Within 10 to 20 minutes of drinking alcohol it will start to affect your body and your mind. Although it is safe for adults to drink alcohol responsibly, in small amounts, drinking too much alcohol can have dangerous results.

How are alcoholic drinks made?

The alcohol in alcoholic drinks is actually a chemical called ethanol. It is possible to make ethanol from almost anything you eat — even potatoes! People place yeast, natural sugars (from grapes, barley, hops, potatoes etc) and water together to ferment and the result is ethanol. To make very strong alcoholic drinks called spirits, people distil the ethanol by heating it up.

Different drinks

Many people enjoy the taste of alcoholic drinks. Some prefer wine, port or sherry, which are all made from grapes or other fruits. Others choose beer or lager, which is made from barley or hops. Cider is made from apples whilst whisky is made from barley. Many younger people try alcopops — sweet drinks mixed with alcohol.

These grapes will be harvested to make wine.

Alcopops mix strong spirits with fruit juice or fizzy drinks, and are popular with young people.

Drinking alcohol is an accepted part of everyday life in many countries.

Alcohol strength

Some drinks are stronger than others because they contain more alcohol. Each can or bottle has a percentage figure printed on it to tell the drinker how much alcohol the drink contains. This number is called the 'proof'. The higher the number, the less someone can drink before the alcohol begins to affect them.

IN FOCUS
Units of alcohol

Alcohol is measured in units. One unit of alcohol is half a pint of beer, a small glass of wine or a measure of whisky. Doctors recommend that women shouldn't drink more than 14 units of alcohol a week, and that men shouldn't drink more than 21. As the full effects of alcohol on young bodies is not yet clear, doctors recommend that young people should drink as little as possible, and certainly less than the recommended units for adult men or women.

ROLE-PLAY: WHAT IS WRONG WITH ALCOPOPS?

With a friend, choose one of the views and follow it through.

1 "I like the taste of alcopops. All my friends drink them."

School student, David Baker

2 "It is easy to get drunk on alcopops as some of them have surprisingly high levels of alcohol in them, and yet they taste like fizzy drinks."

School nurse, Theresa Swift

YOUR CALL Some people think all alcohol should be banned — others think we should be taught about its dangers. What do you think?

5

What happens when you drink alcohol?

**A**t first, an alcoholic drink can make someone feel relaxed, happy and more confident than normal. However, if the drinking continues, the person may start to feel unwell as the alcohol starts to affect their brain and other parts of the body.

Early stages

When people drink alcohol, ethanol goes into their bloodstream and is carried around the body, affecting the brain. After the first happy, relaxed feelings wear off, the drinker may find it difficult to concentrate and may start behaving differently from normal — hugging people or even crying.

Losing control

When people drink too much, they feel dizzy and their speech becomes hard to understand. They may be sick or fall asleep, giving their body a chance to deal with the alcohol. When they wake up, they may not remember what happened when they were drunk.

Alcohol poisoning

If someone drinks much too much, too fast, they could get alcohol poisoning. If this happens, brain cells stop working and the body begins to shut down. If the drinker falls into a deep sleep, called a coma, emergency treatment is needed.

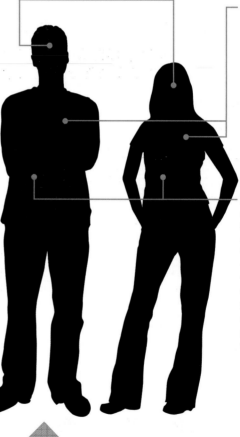

Brain
At first, alcohol can make a person feel happy, but this is often followed by a depressing low. Long-term heavy drinking kills brain cells, and can lead to memory loss and mental problems.

Heart
Drinking a lot of alcohol over a short time can give a person irregular heartbeats, and make them breathless. Long-term heavy drinking can lead to high blood pressure and other heart problems.

Liver
A person's liver can only break down one unit of alcohol per hour. If it has to deal with more than this, it stops working properly. Long-term heavy drinking kills liver cells, and can lead to liver disease.

Alcohol has serious effects on vital body organs, such as the brain, heart and liver.

The more alcohol a person drinks,
the stronger the effect.

A hangover

The after-effects of drinking are known as a 'hangover'. Drinking alcohol makes people need to pass water more than usual, leaving them dehydrated. This gives them a headache, a dry mouth and makes them feel tired. Bright lights and loud noises are painful. Some people will also feel sick or have a stomach upset.

Hangovers can be very unpleasant, and can last for up to two days.

ARGUMENTS FOR AND AGAINST DRINKING ALCOHOL

FOR!

- A small amount of alcohol can be good for your health.
- Drinking can make you feel relaxed and happy.
- Drinking can stop you feeling shy and help you fit in with friends.
- Drinking can help you forget your worries for a while.

AGAINST!

- Drinking too much alcohol, too often, can damage your liver, stomach, heart and brain.
- Drinking too much can make you say or do things you regret afterwards.
- Drinking alcohol can give you bad skin, bad breath and bad teeth, and make you put on weight.
- Getting drunk can put you and other people in danger.

Alcohol in everyday life

In our society, it is normal to drink alcohol. Although alcohol is a drug, it doesn't have the bad reputation held by other drugs, such as tobacco or cannabis. In addition, on television and in films, actors are often shown looking 'cool' and holding a drink. However, the effects of alcohol can be far from cool. These include relatively minor problems — such as bad hangovers — to accidents and crimes linked to drinking alcohol.

People enjoy a drink at a work office party. Many businesses lose money when workers take time off to recover from hangovers caused by over-drinking.

Policing the problems

Although most people drink alcohol responsibly, the police have to deal with many problems caused by people drinking too much alcohol and becoming violent. When crowds gather at football matches or rock festivals, drunkenness can cause trouble. Some people think alcoholic drinks should be banned at all public events, making them safer for everyone to attend.

Picking up the pieces

Hospitals have to deal with many alcohol-related accidents. People who drink and drive are much more likely to cause car accidents. In addition, every weekend, hospitals have to cope with people who have become ill, or fallen and hurt themselves as a result of drinking too much. Some long-term illnesses are caused by drink problems, including liver disease and mental health problems.

The Chinese beer company, Tsingtao, was one of the sponsors of the 2008 Beijing Olympics and saw a huge rise in the sales of its beer as a result of the advertising.

Adverts for alcohol

Adverts for alcohol often show a glamorous lifestyle. They are aimed at encouraging particular groups of people to buy more alcohol, for example women and young people. Some people see no problem with this but others, who are worried about the harm that alcohol can do, think it is wrong to advertise in this way.

Sporting sponsors

Alcoholic drinks companies like to be linked with sport. The companies help pay for stadiums, sponsor major competitions and teams, and in return, get publicity. Some people think sporting organisations should not allow alcohol to be promoted at sporting events, when alcohol can harm people's health. Others think that anything that brings money into sport is a good thing.

YOUR CALL Some people believe that people who have made themselves ill by drinking too much should be forced to pay for their own treatment. Others think everyone should be treated equally. What do you think?

? Dilemma: Josh is captain of his local U13 football team and they need a new set of kit. Josh's father works for a brewery and the brewery will pay for the kit if the team allows the brewery to print its name on the shirts. What should Josh tell his team to do?

Social drinking

People who drink alcohol usually want to relax and enjoy themselves. Alcohol is often served at parties and on special occasions. If people are careful about how much they drink, there doesn't have to be a problem.

Where do people drink?

People drink alcohol in restaurants, cafés, clubs and bars, with or without food. People also drink alcohol at parties, with friends or family. Some people drink at home to unwind after a hard day at work. Others, including some teenagers, gather in parks or other open spaces to drink alcohol.

Licensing laws

Places that sell alcohol, for example pubs, off-licences and supermarkets, need a special licence to trade. Each country has its own laws to control the sale of alcohol. In the UK, it is against the law to sell alcohol to anyone under the age of 18 but in the USA, you have to be 21 to buy alcohol from a shop.

At weddings, it is traditional to drink champagne, to wish the married couple good luck.

YOUR CALL Some people argue that it can be hard for people to know how much alcohol to drink, so it is better not to drink at all. What do you think?

Know your limits

Alcohol has a similar effect on everyone but some people find that alcohol affects them more strongly than others. Drinking alcohol with a meal slows down the rate that the alcohol is absorbed into the body. So, by contrast, people who go out drinking on an empty stomach are more likely to get drunk. Medical research shows that most women take longer to process alcohol than men, and that bigger people can absorb more alcohol than smaller people.

Women can become drunk on a smaller amount of alcohol than men, because their bodies are smaller and their livers do not break down the alcohol as easily.

ROLE PLAY: WHAT'S WRONG WITH ALCOHOL?

These two people disagree about alcohol. With a friend, choose one of the views and follow it through.

1 "Alcohol is a drug, and it should be illegal like other drugs. It kills more people than any other drug – in the USA, one in every 20 deaths is caused by alcohol."

Medical student, Hannah Smithers

2 "In moderation, alcohol is actually good for your health. Some experts say it reduces the risk of heart disease."

Accountant, Simon Chandler

Learning to drink

Some children first taste alcohol with their family, at home during mealtimes. Although it is against the law to sell alcohol to children, it is not illegal for children to drink alcohol in a family environment. Some people think it is good to introduce children to alcohol in this way, but others disagree, saying that it encourages them to start drinking much too young.

Family life

In some European countries, including Italy and Spain, children drink a little wine with their family meal. People argue that this is a good way of learning how to drink small amounts of alcohol, responsibly. Italy and Spain have lower rates of alcohol addiction than the UK and the USA, where fewer children drink at home with their families.

Myth busting

Parents and teachers should help children understand that drinking alcohol will not make them more popular, and that it makes people more likely to have accidents. Children need to know that drinking alcohol does not mix with certain activities, such as driving, using machinery, sport and swimming.

Drinking wine at family meals is common in some European countries.

Although alcohol is easy to pick up in many supermarkets, children are not allowed to purchase alcohol.

 Do you think children who are introduced to alcohol by members of their family are more likely to drink responsibly when they grow up?

ARGUMENTS FOR AND AGAINST LETTING CHILDREN DRINK AT HOME

FOR!

- Letting children drink at home stops alcohol from becoming a temptation when they grow up.
- Responsible drinking at home teaches children a good attitude towards alcohol, and helps them avoid bad drinking habits in the future.

AGAINST!

- Letting children drink alcohol at home encourages them to start drinking when they are too young.
- Parents should have 'zero tolerance' to alcohol, so children know exactly where they stand, and there is no confusion.

ROLE-PLAY: WHO IS RESPONSIBLE?

These two people have different views about children and alcohol. Who do you agree with and why?

1 "If children drink too much, it is always the parents' fault. Children are too young to be responsible."

Computer programmer, Jamila Khan

2 "Children seem to spend more time with their friends than with their families these days. It's impossible for parents to control their drinking."

Security guard, Dave Bench

Under-age drinking

I t is against the law to sell alcohol to young people under a certain age limit, a limit which varies around the world. For example, in France the age limit is 16, in the UK and Australia it is 18, in Japan it is 20, and in the USA it is 21. In many countries young people have to carry identity cards, to prove their age if they want to buy alcohol.

Drinking alcohol can become a habit when young people meet together.

Why do young people drink?

Some children and young people start to drink alcohol because they want to be like their friends. This is called 'peer-group pressure'. They may think that drinking will make them look cool and grown up, because TV, films and adverts often show drinking as fun. Some people believe alcohol advertising should be banned for this reason. Others are just copying what their parents do — when they meet with their friends they feel they need to drink alcohol.

Health risks

Children's bodies are small, so they absorb alcohol quickly, speeding up its effects. In addition, teenage bodies all develop at different rates so it is difficult for doctors to say at which age it is safe to start drinking alcohol. What they do know is that drinking alcohol places a strain on a teenager's undeveloped liver, which has to process poisons (toxins) from the alcohol. Alcohol may also cause permanent damage to parts of the brain that are still developing.

Sport and alcohol do not mix. If you want to play your best, don't drink alcohol.

In the UK, some medical experts recommend that children under the age of 15 should not drink any alcohol at all.

How bad is it?

In the UK, about 35,000 people under the age of 16 drink more than the safe weekly limit for adults. In the USA, nearly two million young people over the age of 12 are being treated for alcohol problems. Since there is no accepted safe alcohol limit for teenagers, those that drink are likely to be inflicting permanent damage on their bodies.

? Dilemma:

12-year-old Franco is at the park, and his friends arrive with some cans of beer. They give him a can to try. Franco says no, but they call him a loser. What should he do?

ROLE PLAY: THE RIGHT AGE

These two people disagree about the minimum age for being allowed to buy alcohol. Who do you think is right?

1 "In the USA, you can't buy alcohol until you are 21 years old. But when you are 18, you can vote, get married and fight a war. If you are old enough for these things, why can't you buy alcohol too?"

US soldier, Private Steven Kirby

2 "Between the ages of 18 and 23, young people's brains are still developing. By the age of 21, you are more able to make sensible decisions about how much to drink."

Student, Li Wei

Binge drinking

Some people drink alcohol to get drunk — this is known as 'binge drinking'. Groups of people who binge drink together claim that this is normal behaviour, and a good laugh. However, their drunken behaviour can often affect other people, and can even endanger lives. An evening that started as a fun night out could end in a bad accident, or trouble with the police.

Binge drinking can end the party fun if people fall asleep from drinking too much.

Drinking to celebrate?

Some people binge drink on special occasions, for example on their birthday, when they want to have a good time. They argue that it is an enjoyable way to relax, and that they are not doing themselves or anyone else any great harm. Some people feel that they haven't had a good time unless they have become drunk.

Health dangers

Regular binge drinking can damage the liver, heart and brain, and can also lead to alcohol addiction. Any attempt to binge drink, even for the first time, may result in alcohol poisoning (see pages 6—7). When people are drunk, they are far more likely to have serious accidents.

Cheap alcohol

Supermarkets sell alcohol very cheaply, with special offers such as 'Buy one, get one free'. Bars and pubs also run 'happy hours' selling alcoholic drinks at cheap prices early in the evening, to bring people into their bar. Some people complain that this encourages binge drinking.

ROLE PLAY: ARE HAPPY HOURS A GOOD IDEA?

These people have different views on happy hours. Who do you agree with?

1 "Happy hours encourage people to drink heavily, early on in the evening, ready to start a long night of drinking. This can lead to violence, and turn town centres into no-go areas late at night."

City resident, Pandit Singh

2 "A happy hour is a business promotion that helps bars make money. It's up to customers to drink and act responsibly during a happy hour."

Bar owner, Frank Watson

 IN FOCUS

Responsible drinking – if you decide to drink, here are some tips

DO eat before you start drinking.
DO drink slowly.
DO space alcoholic drinks out with soft ones.
DO be sure you know what you are drinking.
DO follow rules – don't drink if you're not allowed to.

DON'T drink too much.
DON'T drink too quickly.
DON'T drink for a bet or a competition.
DON'T drink to impress other people.
DON'T drink if you don't want to.

Some people drink a lot of alcohol to keep up with friends. This is not a smart thing to do.

Alcohol and health

Drinking a small amount of alcohol can be good for your health. However, too much alcohol can be a very bad thing. Every day hospitals treat people who have drunk too much. People who drink too much over a long period of time may become seriously ill.

All in moderation

Some medical experts say that moderate drinking can reduce the risk of a heart attack, and may also reduce the risk of having a stroke. It can make people less likely to develop a medical condition called diabetes. This evidence applies to middle-aged and older people. There are no known health benefits from drinking alcohol for young people.

Pregnant women are often advised to avoid alcohol altogether, although some people argue that one or two small glasses of wine a week may be safe.

Liver damage

Years of heavy drinking damage a person's liver, so that it can't work properly. The liver removes alcohol from the body but, over time, the alcohol can kill off liver cells leading to cirrhosis of the liver, hepatitis or liver cancer. A drinker may not realise how damaged their liver is until their health is seriously at risk.

YOUR CALL Some people think heavy drinkers with liver disease should not be given liver transplants. Others believe that life-saving treatment should be offered to everyone, no questions asked. What do you think?

If women drink alcohol while they are pregnant, they risk harming their unborn child. However, some people argue that one or two glasses a week may be perfectly safe.

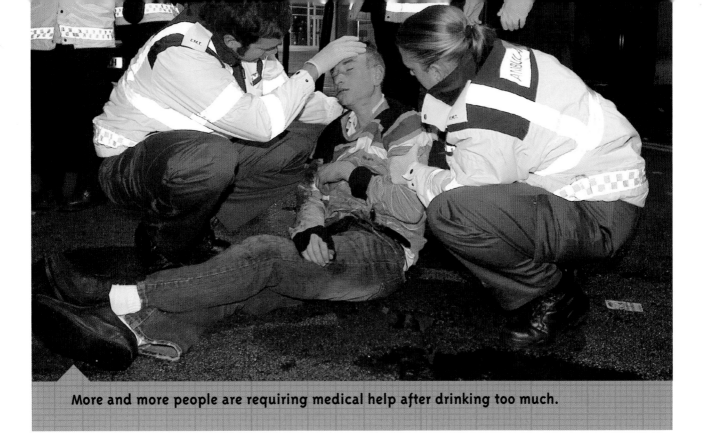

More and more people are requiring medical help after drinking too much.

IN FOCUS

Drink and drugs

It is dangerous to mix drugs of any kind with alcohol. Alcohol can make drugs stronger, and some drugs can increase the effects of alcohol. Other drugs, for example antibiotics, may not work if taken with alcohol, whilst aspirin and paracetamol can damage the body if taken with alcohol.

Serious health risks

People who drink too much may develop heart disease and high blood pressure. They could also develop stomach ulcers and forms of cancer. Drinking too much may cause mental health problems, including depression. Heavy drinkers can suffer memory loss and panic attacks, but they may not connect these symptoms with how much they drink.

Dilemma:

Tom, aged 12, finds a woman lying asleep on the pavement, with an empty bottle of spirits by her side. If she has alcohol poisoning, she could be fighting for her life. In which order should Tom act?

1. Phone for an ambulance.
2. Get someone to help him roll the woman onto her side, so she doesn't choke.
3. Call out for help.

(Answer: 3, 2, 1.)

Addicted to alcohol

Alcoholics are people who are addicted to alcohol. They cannot get through the day without drinking alcohol. Many alcoholics join support groups to get advice, or go to 'rehab' clinics to help them stop drinking. Recovering alcoholics often have to give up alcohol completely, for the rest of their lives.

Why do people become alcoholics?

This is not an easy question to answer. It seems that some people gain more pleasure from drinking alcohol than others, which could lead them to drink more often and become physically dependent on alcohol. Other people turn to alcohol after a stressful event, or because they are worried about something, or feel very lonely. People who grew up in a family where alcohol was a problem, or started to drink when they were very young, are more likely to become addicted to alcohol.

Living with an alcoholic

Living with an alcoholic is extremely difficult. It can mean coping with someone who lies, steals and has violent mood swings. There may be serious health, safety and money worries since it is hard for an alcoholic to hold onto a job. The children of alcoholics sometimes have to care for a parent, as well as the rest of the family.

Physical and mental health

Recovering alcoholics sometimes need hospital treatment for serious health problems. They may also need counselling, to talk through problems that caused the alcoholism in the first place, or that happened because of it.

Some people lose everything when they become addicted to alcohol — their job, their family and their home.

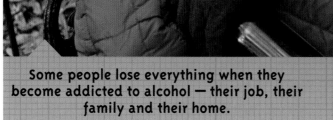

For some alcoholics, the hardest thing is admitting they have a problem with drink. Talking to a counsellor may be the first step.

IN FOCUS

Support groups

Alcoholics can get help from support groups, such as Alcoholics Anonymous or others listed on page 31. For people who are living with an alcoholic, help is at hand from sympathetic groups, also listed on page 31.

YOUR CALL Some people believe that the only way to stop people becoming alcoholics is to ban alcohol, or to make it very expensive. Do you think this would work?

? Dilemma:

Sam thinks that his school friend Mark is becoming dependant on alcohol. Whenever they are out with friends, Mark gets drunk. Sam thinks Mark is drinking alone at home as well. How could he help Mark?

ROLE-PLAY: WHOSE PROBLEM?

Take one of these arguments and follow it through.

1
"The government should spend more money on supporting alcoholics and their families. This will improve society, for example, by reducing the problems of family breakdown, violence and homelessness."

Social worker, Gillian Lever

2
"Alcoholics cause their own problems, so they should be left alone to sort them out. The government shouldn't spend money on helping them."

Fitness instructor, Jim Edwards

Alcohol and the law

There are many laws concerning alcohol. Different countries have different laws, and some even ban alcohol altogether, for religious and cultural reasons. However, most countries allow alcohol to be sold and drunk but try to control how it is used.

People who sell alcohol are allowed to ask for an ID card to prove the age of someone who is buying a drink.

Minimum age

In most countries, it is illegal to sell alcohol to people under a certain age. If a pub, restaurant or shop breaks the minimum age law, their licence to sell alcohol could be taken away and the business closed down.

Drink-driving

It is against the law to drive after drinking too much alcohol. If the police find that a driver has drunk more than the legal limit, they will take him or her to court. Punishments vary from a big fine, to a short driving ban or a prison sentence, if somebody has been hurt or killed.

Drinking in public

In the USA and Australia, someone can be arrested for drinking alcohol in a public place. In the UK the police have the right to remove alcohol from someone who is drinking in public. There are various laws to control drunkenness in public.

These people have different opinions. Who do you think is right?

1 "If bars are open for longer, people take their time and don't drink too much, too quickly. This means fewer people get dangerously drunk."

City banker, Daniel Ward

2 "If bars are open for a short time, people drink less, so they don't get so drunk."

Police officer, Carol Macintosh

Tax on alcohol

Most governments place a tax on alcohol. This means that money from the sale of each drink or bottle of alcohol goes to the government, and can be used to sort out problems caused by alcohol. The higher alcohol prices also put some people off drinking in the first place.

IN FOCUS

Prohibition

Between 1919 and 1933, the US government banned all trade in alcohol. They wanted to please people who believed alcohol was wrong, and also wanted to ease food shortages by using all available grain to feed people. The ban backfired, crime got worse and alcohol was still made and sold illegally. Eventually the law returned to how it was.

Government agents destroy bottles of alcohol during Prohibition in 1920s America.

Drink-driving

Driving a car after drinking too much alcohol is very dangerous. Alcohol affects the brain and makes a driver more likely to take risks. Alcohol also slows down reactions and blurs vision. Every year, many thousands of people are killed by drink-drivers.

Some groups of friends take it in turns to be the driver — and that person does not drink alcohol on the evening that they are the driver.

Legal limits

The amount of alcohol that drivers are allowed to have in their blood is called the 'Blood Alcohol Concentration', or BAC. Some people try to persuade governments to pass tougher laws, to reduce this limit. They believe this would cut the drink-driving death toll.

Over the limit?

Different people can drink varying amounts of alcohol before they are 'over the limit'. If an adult drinks over two pints of beer, they have probably got too much alcohol in their blood. But some people are over the limit if they drink less, or under the limit if they drink more. It depends on many factors including how much food they have eaten, how their body breaks down alcohol and how big they are.

Risks to young people

Young people who have just learned to drive are most likely to be involved in alcohol-related road accidents. Even a small amount of alcohol in the blood could affect the driving skills of inexperienced drivers. If they drink too much, they may kill or injure themselves, or other innocent people. Some people think it should be illegal for young drivers to drink anything at all.

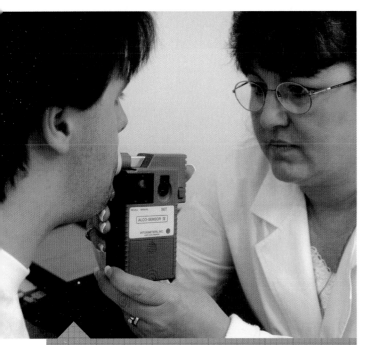

If the result of a breathalyser test (above) is unclear, the driver may have to give a blood test.

YOUR CALL Your friend's mum offers to drive you home but she has been drinking wine. Should you get in the car, or refuse and risk upsetting her?

IN FOCUS

Breathalyser

Drivers who are suspected of being over the legal alcohol limit in the UK, Australia and USA can be stopped by police and asked to blow into a breathalyser. This instrument measures the amount of alcohol in the blood.

ROLE-PLAY: SHOULD DRIVERS DRINK AT ALL?

These people disagree about drink-driving. Who do you agree with?

1 "If you drink alcohol, you can't be sure how it will affect you or how close you are to the limit. It's not worth the risk. I never drink if I am going to drive."

Nurse, Shaila Patel

2 "As long as people don't go over the limit, it's OK to drink and drive. It's not against the law if you're under the limit."

Waitress, Sarah Flynn

Alcohol and violence

Alcohol affects the way that people behave. It can change their mood and alter their reactions, often in a bad way. People who have drunk too much can suddenly get angry, start arguments and fights, and refuse to back down from them. This can result in injury and pain.

Some people blame alcohol for the rise in violence in city centres.

Street violence

The abuse of alcohol can lead to violence. Groups of binge drinkers sometimes cause trouble on the streets of a town or city. Innocent passers-by may be threatened, or even hurt. If the drinkers are carrying weapons, such as knives, this can end in tragedy.

Football hooligans

Hooliganism at sports events is a problem in some European countries and is often fuelled by alcohol. Some people think sports fans should be banned from attending a match if they are carrying alcohol, or have already been drinking.

Domestic violence

Heavy drinkers may become aggressive towards their family. Violence in the home is often called domestic violence. Support organisations, helplines and websites help all victims of domestic violence — see page 31.

ROLE-PLAY: SHOULD ALCOHOL BE BANNED AT SPORTS EVENTS?

Who do you agree with and why?

1 "Alcohol should be banned at football matches. It causes nothing but trouble and puts innocent people at risk."

Newsagent, Greg Sparks

2 "People have the right to drink when and where they like. People should be trusted to act responsibly."

Football fan, Charlie Mardell

? Dilemma:
Harry's friend has told him a secret. He says that his father hits him when he returns from the pub. Harry has seen bruises on his friend's body. If Harry tells his parents this information they will probably contact the school, or the social services. What should Harry do?

YOUR CALL In some busy places, street violence is a growing problem, making people afraid to go out at night. Do you think alcohol should be banned in these places, or severely restricted?

Domestic violence is always wrong, and people affected by it should get help.

Alcohol in different cultures

There is nothing new about alcohol — there is evidence that people in prehistoric times fermented fruit to make alcoholic drinks. Many cultures around the world today accept alcohol in society whilst others consider it to be a growing threat.

A healthy choice?

In countries that have a tradition of producing wine, such as France, wine is often drunk with meals. Red wine, in particular, is thought to be good for health when drunk with food, lowering cholesterol levels and reducing heart disease. The French enjoy some of the longest lifespans in Europe.

Changing society

Alcohol is becoming more of a problem in some societies, including the UK, where binge drinking is increasingly common. Drunken behaviour can cause serious damage to people and the places where they live. Liver disease is on the rise in the UK, even among people who are only in their 20s and 30s.

Alcohol is a traditional part of life in some countries, such as Germany.

Who do you agree with?

1 "Alcohol should be banned, because it destroys lives. Many fatal accidents are caused by alcohol. It may be hard for society to change but a world without alcohol would be safer and happier."

Ambulance driver, Davina Justice

2 "You can't stop people from drinking alcohol if they want to. Instead, governments should find better ways of controlling alcohol, and facing up to the problems it causes."

Teacher, Owen Morgan

Alcohol ban

Alcohol is banned for religious reasons in some countries in the Middle East, such as Saudi Arabia and Kuwait. Despite the ban, some people still drink in secret, risking imprisonment if they are caught. When people want to drink alcohol, it is hard to stop them.

IN FOCUS

Avoiding alcohol

Under Islamic law, Muslims are not allowed to drink alcohol. But Islam is not the only religion to reject alcohol. It is also avoided by many Sikhs, Buddhists and some Christians. Many people of no religious faith also decide not to drink alcohol. This may be for personal reasons, such as health problems, or because they have had a bad experience with it.

These people are at a Muslim wedding. There is no alcohol at the celebrations, but this does not stop everyone from enjoying themselves.

RESEARCH IT YOURSELF

Find out more about: attitudes to alcohol in Islam, Sikhism, Buddhism and Christianity.

Glossary

addiction	Being so dependent on something, it is hard to give it up.
alcohol poisoning	A dangerous physical reaction to an overdose of alcohol.
alcoholic	Someone who is addicted to alcohol.
binge drink	Drink alcohol with the intention of getting drunk.
Blood Alcohol Concentration (BAC)	The amount of alcohol in a person's blood.
breathalyser	An instrument a person blows into, to find out the level of alcohol in their blood.
coma	A deep state of unconsciousness.
counselling	Professional help to deal with a problem.
dehydrated	Experiencing a loss of fluid in the body.
depression	An illness that involves the body, mood and thoughts, and changes how a person feels and thinks.
domestic violence	Physical abuse that takes place in a person's home.
drug	A substance used to treat an illness or change a person's mood.
drunk	Experiencing the effects of drinking too much alcohol.
hangover	The after-effects on the body of drinking too much alcohol.
happy hour	The time of day when a bar sells cheap alcoholic drinks, often early in the evening.
hooliganism	Behaviour that involves drunken and destructive violence.
identity card	A card that proves who somebody is, and how old they are.
legal limit	The maximum amount of something that is allowed by law.
minimum age	The youngest age a person can be to do a particular thing.
off-licence	A shop selling alcohol, for people to drink somewhere else.
panic attack	A sudden feeling of fear, and extreme anxiety.
peer-group pressure	A person's desire to do or have the same things as their friends.
Prohibition	A period of American history between 1919 and 1933, when it was illegal to buy or sell alcohol.
proof	Alcoholic proof is the amount of alcohol in a particular drink.
rehab clinic	A place where people go to recover from an addiction.
spirits	Very strong alcoholic drinks.
tobacco	Dried leaves of the tobacco plant, smoked in cigarettes.
toxin	A poisonous substance.
unit	Alcohol is measured in units — one unit is 10ml in volume, or 8g in weight.
zero tolerance	Refusal to tolerate a particular kind of behaviour, such as drug abuse.

Further information

Websites

United Kingdom
www.talktofrank.com
www.drinkaware.co.uk
Two good UK websites, which give helpful information and offer support for young people and adults on the subject of alcohol and related problems.

www.adfam.org.uk
www.addaction.org.uk
Two practical UK websites that offer help and support for anyone who is living with an alcoholic, or has a drink problem themselves.

www.childline.org.uk
www.thehideout.org.uk
Two very useful UK websites that offer a confidential helpline, with support and advice to children and young people dealing with domestic violence.

www.alcoholics-anonymous.org.uk
This UK website offers information and advice for people addicted to alcohol, with a national helpline number and contact details of local support groups.

United States
www.thecoolspot.gov
A good US website for young people, with information, help and advice about alcohol and how to deal with peer-group pressure.

www.aa.org
This US website offers information and advice for people addicted to alcohol, with a directory of local support groups.

Australia
www.reachout.com.au
A practical Australian website aimed at young people, giving information about alcohol and other drugs, with a helpline offering help and support.

New Zealand
www.hadenough.org.nz
A helpful New Zealand website that gives general information about alcohol, with useful web links and helpline numbers.

Note to parents and teachers: Every effort has been made by the Publishers to ensure that these websites are suitable for children, that they are of the highest educational value, and that they contain no inappropriate or offensive material. However, because of the nature of the Internet, it is impossible to guarantee that the contents of these sites will not be altered. We strongly advise that Internet access is supervised by a responsible adult.

Index

These are the lists of contents for each title in *Your Call:*

Alcohol
What is alcohol? • What happens when you drink alcohol? • Alcohol in everyday life • Social drinking • Learning to drink • Under-age drinking • Binge drinking • Alcohol and health • Addicted to alcohol • Alcohol and the law • Drink-driving • Alcohol and violence • Alcohol in different cultures

Animal Rights
About animal rights • Eating animals • Wearing fur • Farm animals • Hunting and fishing • Culling • Working animals • Sporting and circus animals • Zoos and safari parks • Pets • Animal research • Breeding and pedigree • Endangered animals

Being A Vegetarian
What is a vegetarian? • What is a vegan? • Animal welfare • Green vegetarians • Feeding the world • The healthy choice? • A balanced diet Vegetarian children • Read the label • Going vegetarian • Clothes and make-up • Extreme vegetarians • Vegetarianism around the world

Bullying
What is bullying? • Why do people bully? • Emotional bullying • Verbal bullying • Physical bullying • Cyber bullying • Racist bullying • Bullying at home • Bullying at school • Bullying in sport • Stop the bullying! • Being a witness • Anti-bullying groups

Campaigning for Change
Why do people campaign for change? • Lobbying and pressure groups • Demonstrations, marches and rallies • Publicity stunts • Big events • Charities • Media campaigns • Local campaigns • Raising awareness • Campaign labels and marks • Modern technology • Extremists • Getting involved

Gangs
About gangs • Why people join gangs • Looking alike • Group behaviour • Peaceful gangs • Violent gangs • Girl gangs • Turf wars • Knife crimes • Gun crimes • Social crimes • Safer streets • Youth projects